The Inner Agreement:

A New Approach to Depression and Panic Disorder

By Dale E. Victorine

ISBN: 978-1479289264

Cover photography by Dale E. Victorine

Printed in the United States of America

ACKNOWLEDGMENTS

For faith and inspiration, I'd like to thank Jane DiGirolomo, Robert Mills, and Sheila O'Quirke; and in memoriam, Theda M. Victorine, (my mother), Andrew A. Victorine (my father), and Ruth Gabriel, a wonderful musician, artist, and true friend.

"In each of us there is another whom we do not know."
— Carl G. Jung

CONTENTS

INTRODUCTION

INTRODUCTION

This book is about my own experience with depression and panic disorder, and a technique I stumbled upon that was stunningly transformative for me. For the record, I am not a psychologist or psychotherapist, and do not have a degree in psychology. The technique I'm referring to involves self-hypnosis, communication with one's unconscious mind, visualization, and the use of specific objects.

First, I will discuss briefly the history of thought concerning the unconscious mind – also known popularly as the *subconscious mind*.

Chapter two is an overview of Panic Disorder and Depression.

In chapter three, I describe *my* background, and the various threads of thought and experiences that led to my personal discovery.

Chapter four will explain self-hypnosis and lay out the basic technique I'll call from now on "The Inner Agreement" - which you will have with your unconscious mind.

Chapter five will be an example self-hypnotic session – including The Inner Agreement – to help you plan your own session, or make a recording that you can listen to for your own session – tailored to your specific needs.

Chapter six explains a supplemental technique for communication with the unconscious mind using finger signals.

Chapter seven discusses the importance of mental imagery and visualization in understanding the unconscious mind.

Chapter eight looks at other traditions where objects are important, in order to differentiate between them from the objects that will be used as a result of The Inner Agreement.

Chapter nine looks at some recent brain/mind research that supports The Inner Agreement method.

Finally, chapter ten is devoted to reflections on my experiences with this technique, its meanings, and ramifications – again based on my relative layman's knowledge of psychology.

Chapter One

The Unconscious Mind and The Inner Agreement

We all know that the unconscious mind is an important part of our thinking process, and a major focus for most psychological theories and therapies. Freud first formally proposed the idea of an unconscious mind, and formulated a method that had patients spending years in therapy.

But what if the unconscious mind were not as complicated as it seems? What if its basic desires were extremely simple, and all it wanted to do is *"its job"* – if only the *conscious* mind would make an effort to acknowledge it, and try to satisfy its simple requests? And what if, once this bridge was established, our thinking became much more clear, and problem solving much easier?

The history of psychology is filled with countless pages on the unconscious mind, and theories on how to understand and master it; but one thing is clear: The unconscious mind stores vast amounts of memories, and information we've learned. Unfortunately, an unconscious mind that is not in tune with its conscious counterpart will have difficulties in organizing this information; and may dwell obsessively on the most painful memories, stuck in an endless loop.

For Sigmund Freud, the unconscious was, to a large extent, a realm of repressed thoughts, and the self struggled to keep those thoughts repressed in order to avoid the disturbing things hidden there – mainly sexual in nature.

Carl Jung divided the unconscious into two parts: the personal, and the collective unconscious. Though his ideas about the personal unconscious were similar to Freud's, his concept of the collective unconscious suggested a profound element in our psyche that has inherited psychic structures and archetypal experiences. In other words, a knowledge that goes beyond our limited realm of experience and upbringing - a knowledge based on symbols that reaches back into our deepest past as a species.

Primitive man, too, had an unconscious mind. But he also had a different way of thinking about, and seeing the world than modern man does. He was not so divided. He did not live in a world where people are expected to be completely rational – a "brave new world" where all symbolic meaning is cast aside in exchange for gadgets, and a headlong dash for financial wealth.

For primitive man, things could be both object and subject – both real and symbolic. The very stones were alive, and the gods looked down on him from the sky. So, should it be any surprise that the unconscious mind experiences the world differently from the conscious mind? For example, it's a well known fact that the unconscious mind deals mainly in images.

This book presents a way of rediscovering a part of our mind that hasn't changed for millennia, and is unlikely to change any time soon. As technologically and intellectually advanced as we think we are, we are still brought up short by our own refusal to accept the needs and special language of our own inner selves.

On the face of it, the goal and outcome of my technique might seem deceptively simple: *Let the unconscious mind show what it desires – perhaps a common object is all. Obtain that object (which you may already have), and keep it around at least part of the time - or until such a time as the unconscious mind no longer seems to need it.* But what is really happening is the beginning of an *inner agreement* – the opening of an inner dialogue that can lead to transformed relationships, freedom from the pain of depression and anxiety, clearer thinking, and a renewed zest for life. Because of this process, the unconscious mind's mysterious needs are met, and because it no longer is crying out to be heard, it spontaneously realigns and returns to a healthy and contented state. Your problems won't disappear, but you'll feel much more capable of solving them.

Chapter Two

Depression and Panic Disorder

Depression

This book and the technique I describe focuses on Depression and Panic Disorder – because these are problems I've dealt with personally, and have experienced great improvement first hand using my method. Yes, I was my own guinea pig.

According to Wikipedia, "Depression is a state of low mood and aversion to activity that can have a negative effect on a person's thoughts, behavior, feelings, world view and physical well-being. Depressed people may feel sad, anxious, empty, hopeless, worried, helpless, worthless, guilty, irritable, hurt or restless. They may lose interest in activities that once were pleasurable, experience loss of appetite or overeating, have problems concentrating, remembering details, or making decisions and may contemplate or attempt suicide. Insomnia, excessive sleeping, fatigue, loss of energy, or aches, pains or digestive problems that are resistant to treatment may also be present."

Depression is often treated with drugs, if treated at all. So many people suffer silently because of various factors: cultural, financial, etc. Depression's severity can range from mild to severe, and is the main cause of virtually all suicide.

I've read that depression is anger turned inward. I disagree with this idea. I believe, after experiencing it myself, and coming to a major realization about it, that depression is caused when the unconscious mind loses hope that the conscious mind will, in any way, discover what the unconscious mind needs on a deep level. The unconscious mind gives up. I'll go so far to say that if the unconscious mind cannot find a reason to believe in the future, then depression is inevitable.

But you might think, what could the unconscious mind actually want then? That's the question. But there's no need to go down a list of thousands of possibilities, including, unfortunately, medication. The unconscious mind isn't expected to solve complex life problems all by itself. That's why the

6

conscious mind developed. But the unconscious mind still has its simple needs, and the key is to allow it to show them to us.

I feel I stumbled across a way to do that - A way to acknowledge a deep and ancient part of our psyche. The result will be startlingly simple, but could lead to a dramatic shift in mood. Then the conscious mind would be clearer and more able to face the problems at hand.

Panic Disorder

Panic disorder involves uncontrollable feelings of anxiety and fear, with no apparent reason or cause. We evolved with a built-in survival strategy when faced with danger. Adrenaline would be released and we would decide very quickly whether to flee or stand our ground and fight. But nowadays we very rarely find ourselves facing a predator. And yet, many of us experience all of the symptoms of a life or death encounter. Panic attacks can be debilitating and frightening events. You may even feel as if you're about to die.

We've come a long way from the dangerous world in which we evolved. But perhaps we've left behind too much of our earlier selves in the mad rush to the future. We've forgotten that we started out with a mind that dealt with things in its own way. In order to come down from the trees and live on the plains, we developed very special tools. And we developed weapons to increase our chances of survival.

Our modern lives are extremely stressful in their way. We're not being attacked by a saber-toothed cat, but we're worried about job, money, sex, health, marriage, our kids – the list is endless. We live in a complex world that's getting more complex every day. No wonder many of us begin to get stuck in "flight" mode – but there's nowhere to run. Early man had something though, to help him feel more secure: a weapon. Now I'm not saying that we should be carrying a gun, spear, etc. But I found that a small, mostly symbolic object that somehow represented that primal tool of protection helped alleviate most of my symptoms of panic disorder. And that, to me was a tall order. In chapter three I tell, to the best of my ability that story.

Chapter Three

My Background and Discovery

I'd have to say that first and foremost, I'm a composer. I've been writing classically oriented music since high school, and am largely self-taught. I'm active in two organizations that present concerts of new music by local composers in the Monterey and San Francisco Bay areas. I play the flute, piano and guitar, and make renaissance flutes. I'm also an apartment manager in San Jose, Ca.

I became interested in psychology in my late teens, partly because of a desire to understand my own moods, and partly because of a fascination with the human mind and creativity. At the same time I became intensely interested in spirituality and dreams. Some of the books I read were about Gestalt Psychology, self-hypnosis, altered states of consciousness, out-of-body experiences, lucid dreams, and ESP.

As a young person, I was a shy, and found it somewhat hard to make friends. After a couple short, but intense bouts with depression, I tried some self-hypnosis to try to search my memories for the source of the present feelings. This helped somewhat, but it was clear that it wasn't a solution in itself. I was prescribed a medication at one point, but refused to continue taking it because it made me feel strange and interfered with my creativity.

Through my 20s and early 30s those times when I was depressed seemed to be when I was having relationship, or job problems, but I muddled through and always seemed to have enough creativity to keep composing.

In 1989 I met my wife, Banyen, who was from Thailand. We met at work in America, and after she returned to Thailand with her co-workers, we corresponded and I moved to Thailand in 1990. We soon married, and I lived there for three years teaching English.

We returned to America in 1994 with our daughter, Sandra. Our son, Stephen, was born in1996. We eventually moved to San Jose in 1998 to be closer to my brothers and mother, and I took a job as apartment manager.

Stress at work and financial worries took a toll, and I often found myself depressed and anxious. I had already had one clear panic attack in my mid 20s – a racing heart, but at that time this isolated incident was inexplicable and eventually largely forgotten.

Now there often was a pervasive feeling of anxiety and mild depression. This caused problems at home and at work with, for one thing, irritability and outbursts of temper. Fortunately, I didn't become physically abusive, though. Other symptoms included intestinal irritability, and a recurring ache in my lower right abdomen.

In 2007 I had my first serious panic attack. After getting up from an early evening nap I felt strangely faint. I couldn't shake the feeling that I was about to pass out. My wife took me to the ER, and at first they thought I might be having a heart attack. The cardiologist came in and found nothing wrong with the EKG. I was admitted for one night and given a stress test, but nothing was wrong with my heart. That, at least, was some comfort.

I went home not knowing any more about what had really happened than when I went to the ER. But it slowly dawned on me after some reflection, and reading some things online, that I might have had a panic attack.

This next part might make it look like I have a drinking problem, but I can assure you that I drink in moderation. The next time I felt the same feeling of faintness, I tried having a small amount of whiskey, and I found that the feeling went away in a few minutes. This made me positive that the feeling was being caused by anxiety.

I began researching panic disorder and the various treatments – both with psychotherapy and drugs. When I went to my doctor and described the incident, he suggested that I try one medication. I did, but chose not to continue, because the side effects (lack of creativity, night sweats, flat emotions, etc.) were not worth it. I decided to soldier on and deal with this problem the best I could.

A few months later, while visiting friends out of town, I had an episode that was much worse. I had intense chills for several hours during the night, as if I had a fever, and my thoughts became a complete jumble.

In 2008 a thought occurred to me that involved self-hypnosis, and special approach to my unconscious mind. What if I asked my unconscious mind to tell or show me what it wanted? I already knew that the unconscious mind deals mainly in pictures and symbols, so I tried this: I put myself into a self-hypnotic trance, and then asked my unconscious mind to show me what it needed to feel *safer*. I then told it I would count to 10 and wait for an answer. (In the next chapter I will go into this process in more detail.) After counting slowly to 10, I waited. The thought and image came that I should carry a pocket knife in one of my pants pockets.

I remembered that in one of my dreams from early childhood, someone had handed me an assortment of pocketknives of various colors, and that I'd been deeply disappointed on waking that I didn't really have them. Perhaps there is something primal about having a knife, as ancient man was able to make such great advances because of his ability to use tools – especially knives.

The experiment continued – and I chose one of my favorite pocket knives and began to carry it regularly. I'd always had a pocket knife or two, and had collected more over the years, but didn't actually carry one very often.

To my amazement, there was a very rapid change. The panic attacks largely abated, and several other long term problems quickly improved or went away. I'd picked and bitten my lower lip for years, and this behavior almost completely stopped. I found that I was less anxious, and more patient with people and stressful situations. Also certain situations that shouldn't have been stressful in the first place lost their stressfulness. One thing I realized was that to cope with certain stressful or anxious feelings, I'd sometimes been compensating by getting angry instead.

I saw that, while other treatments try to impose authoritative belief systems on the unconscious mind, or numb it with drugs; I had treated it with respect and given it a chance to speak.

Let me be clear about one thing: This object – in my case, a pocket knife – was not something I would go into a panic about if I didn't have it with me. It was as if 90% of the change occurred because I'd taken the time to "hear out" my unconscious mind, and make an effort to satisfy its needs.

In 2010 I noticed that I was experiencing more depression, and that my creativity was much lower than normal. After spending more than half the year with very few respites, I decided to try my technique again, but with depression as the subject. With this intention, I did my self-hypnosis again and asked my unconscious mind to show me what it wanted. Wearing a wristwatch came to mind, and I remembered how much my first wristwatch meant to me at the age of about 8. Again, I owned several wristwatches, but rarely wore one regularly.

Because of my extra duties (besides running the apartment office) of some maintenance and painting, I was always taking it off. So I had let all of their batteries run down. After replacing the batteries and putting one on, again the effect was almost immediate. My mood lifted, and the incessant dark cloud that I couldn't seem to escape dissipated.

It seems that for me, the watch is both a tool for telling time, and a symbol that helps place me *in* time. Again, didn't "primitive" man spend much of his time seeking to know his place in time, and the scheme of things? To be at one with time and the seasons was not an abstract thing for him. It was essential.

I know some might say that my "therapy" is simple minded, and that they would feel silly carrying whatever their unconscious mind asked for, but maybe this very kind of thinking illustrates how far we've gotten away from living and being at one with the different parts of our own psyches.

Chapter Four

Self-Hypnosis and the Inner Agreement

The state of hypnosis is not one of deep mental relaxation. Though the body may be very relaxed, hypnosis requires the mind to be alert and focused on one object, goal, or thought.

I have only a few experiences with being hypnotized by someone else, and would say that there is more room for straying from the truth when someone else is making the suggestions and leading your mind in certain directions. If the Inner Agreement process is to be facilitated by someone else, that person should fully understand the goals, and only be there to keep the subject focused on the inner process. Ideally, though, I feel that if one wants to be successful with this process, they should learn how to do *self-hypnosis*, or prepare a recording that they can listen to.

My process for self-hypnosis is this: I lie down on my back and make sure I won't be too warm or cold. I try to make sure it's quiet, and that I won't be disturbed. So cell phones need to be turned off and landline phones unplugged if possible.

I close my eyes and begin counting backwards from 50 or 30. The counting should be interspersed with statements like, "I'm becoming more and more relaxed" or "I'm going deeper and deeper". I imagine that I'm as still as a statue, and as immobile. After reaching "zero" I think, "Now, inner self, please show me what I can give you to help you feel safer" (in the case of panic disorder) or "happier" (in the case of depression). "I will count to 10 and wait for you to show me what you need".

I would then count slowly to 10, keeping my mind as blank as possible. It's important to have a patient attitude and expect to get an idea or image. Finally, once a clear image comes (and you will *know* when you have your answer) you could say a mental "thank you" to your unconscious mind.

To come out of the trance, you can think, "I will now count to 5, and when I reach 5 I'll be ready to get up and be fully alert". When you reach 5, stretch your arms and legs, open your eyes, and get up, just as if you were getting up in the morning.

Chapter Five

Example Self-hypnotic Session for use with The Inner Agreement

INTRODUCTION

Welcome to your Inner Agreement exploration session. We'll be seeking to have a direct meeting with the unconscious mind within us. This mind is every bit as powerful and influential as the conscious mind, but over the millennia, we have, to a large part, ceased to know how to communicate with it, or let it show us what it desires to function smoothly.

The unconscious mind was the first to develop, and will always have an important place in our mental and emotional lives. It *can* communicate with us verbally, but prefers to communicate with images. Primitive man had a natural balance between the symbolic and the concrete.

Objects were both real and symbolic at the same time. Early man's first need, besides food and shelter, was safety. The tools he first created were not just for hunting and preparing food. They protected him from threats, when his strength alone would not have been enough.

That is why my theory for Anxiety Disorder is that the unconscious mind will want a both symbolic and practical object that would be useful for self defense. In my case, my unconscious mind showed me a particular pocket knife that I had, and that I should carry it in my pocket. The fact that I did this at all had a tremendous effect on reducing my anxiety and anxiety symptoms. It was not a mental crutch, as it didn't feel necessary to have it with me all the time.

Early man's next leap - to me – was to learn to plan ahead, and so exist in time. As the conscious mind developed, the subconscious mind looked to it for leadership and direction. The conscious mind helped organize things in time and helped with long term planning. The environment where humans developed must have been very changeable, or this kind of leap would not have been necessary.

An animal bonds with a human most closely when it can trust

the human, and the human's behavior. It's the same for the unconscious mind. It has a strong need to feel that the conscious mind is running the show, and knows what to do. For the unconscious mind, the future doesn't have to be perfect, as long as the conscious mind is dependable and planning things thoughtfully.

Lack of faith in the conscious mind to perform this function causes the unconscious mind to "lose hope". Thus, the inexplicable despair that is called depression.

For me, the object that my unconscious mind desired was a wristwatch. I already had several wristwatches, but chose one I liked the most, and wore it more often, and with intent. This had an equally strong effect on my depression. Although the effects of these deliberate choices to satisfy an internal request were clear, it still took 2 to 3 more years to reach a point where there was a truly clear sense of permanent change.

The wristwatch (which included month and day), for me, was both a symbolic and real tool that showed my unconscious mind that I was serious about planning and organizing my time.

Other objects I've tried have had possibly some effect on my psyche, but it's hard to tell for sure.

The key form of the question you will pose to your unconscious mind is, "What can I give you to help you feel...." For anxiety, the end would be "safer", and for depression, "more hopeful".

These changes have not brought a sense of idle contentment, but rather helped me be more active, confident, and clear about myself. I'm a composer, and none of this has any detrimental effect on my creativity.

The next section is an example hypnotic Inner Agreement session. It will give you a framework for developing your own self-hypnotic sessions.

Inner Agreement Session

So now, let's get ready to meet the unconscious mind on its own terms. We'll be using hypnosis, and visualization for this. Find a comfortable place to lie. Make sure that you have a blanket if you feel you'll start to get cold after a few minutes. Lie on your back and begin to relax. Focus on your breathing. Release your thoughts as you relax your body completely.

Stretch and relax your feet and ankles. Stretch and relax your legs. Breathe deeply and more slowly. Imagine that you are slowly becoming a reclining statue in a serene ancient city. You are able to move if you wish, but right now you feel no desire to. You feel extremely still and yet very aware of your body.

We will begin to count backward from thirty to zero, relaxing more and more with each count: 30, 29, 28, 27, you are relaxing more and more....0

Now prepare to ask your question. For anxiety you could ask, "Inner self, what can I give you to help you feel safer?" For depression you could ask, "Inner self, what can I give you to help you feel more hopeful?" Ask your question; then say, "I will count to ten, then wait patiently for you to show me an image for your answer. Let's give this phase five full minutes. Begin now with your question.

Now that you've had a chance to ask your inner self your question, we'll take the answer and return to normal waking consciousness. On the count of ten you'll be refreshed, alert, and ready to continue with your daily activities.

One, two, three – stretch your legs – four, five, six – stretch your arms and breathe deeply – seven, eight – stretch your whole body – nine, ten. You're now back to normal consciousness.

Now think about the answer you received from your unconscious mind, and begin to think of how you can best comply with the request.

This ends your Inner Agreement Session.

Chapter Six

Finger Signals in Communication with The Unconscious Mind

A useful technique I learned years ago from a book on self-hypnosis is the use of finger signals. This can be helpful in situations where the communication with your unconscious mind is based on yes/no answers.

While in a state of hypnosis, you would ask your unconscious mind to express an "yes" answer by moving a particular finger. Once you've double checked this response, you would ask for the finger signal for a "no" answer.

This form of communication can be useful in interfacing with the unconscious, because it can eventually be used while wide awake, and helps reinforce your conscious knowledge of unconscious needs and desires. It's not a substitute for the process I'm calling The Inner Agreement, though – because that process uncovers a specific object, through the receiving of an image. But finger signals can help confirm the choice of a particular object.

Let me add a note of caution here for those who are interested in psychic exploration. There is no way to be sure that this form of communication with the unconscious mind will yield anything more than a reflection of the workings of your *own* unconscious mind. Those who would try to "get" more information than that could be playing games with themselves – and could be in danger of falling into deluded thinking.

I'm not completely against psychic exploration, but using this finger signal method is not advised. Any form of psychic exploration that involves the unconscious mind should be left to those who have gotten strong validation from a variety of sources that they are indeed gifted in this area. The rest of us would have the kind of experience that kids have when playing with a OUIJA board.

Respect your unconscious mind. It has power and pride, though it has relinquished some of its dominance to the "newer" conscious mind. It had to – to survive. Communication with the unconscious mind needs to be a very predictable and controlled process - or, believe me, it *will* take you down the "rabbit hole".

Chapter Seven

Visualization and the Unconscious Mind

One of the obstacles to our being in better touch with our inner selves is that the conscious mind deals more in words and concepts, while the unconscious mind deals more in images and feelings – and a sense of *the totality*. So communicating with the unconscious mind is like relearning a language we knew well when we were very young: The visual language.

Try remembering a fond childhood memory. A scene will probably come to mind. You'll *feel* the place and time of day. You'll see the faces of your friends, teachers, etc. Maybe not with complete accuracy, but your mind will reconstruct the scene. You may not remember much of what was said, but the images will still "speak" to you.

That's why it's so important to develop the art of "hearing" what your unconscious mind is trying to tell you. What it needs to say will be in pictures.

The unconscious mind has a lot of work to do. It's busy taking care of more mental and physical tasks than you'll ever fully know. So you need to approach it on its own terms. The conscious mind, being a more recent evolutionary development, thinks that it runs the show. But it's really only aware of a small part of what is going on in the brain. A recent book that explains how much work the brain does is: *Incognito – The Secret Lives of the Brain*, by David Eagleman. I highly recommend it.

Some people are more visual than others. So some may find the path inwards easier to tread. For those of us who are less visual, I've included a self hypnotic approach. This gently forces us to slow down and focus inwardly. Outer stimuli are minimized, and the inner movie screen can begin to come alive.

Here is something I wrote in 1997 that suggests the way we should approach the unconscious mind:

If you must come to the sea...

After just a minute's walk from school, I sit down in the morning sun, between the gently lapping ocean and the foot path. Those passing by---walking dogs, jogging, cycling, marching steadily--seem curiously driven forward and uninterested in the mysterious universe of sand and water whose edge they skirt. The crying gulls seem either to be laughing, or else warning the uninitiated to keep their distance. For if you must come to the sea, then be prepared to leave your words behind--like the scattered and useless furniture that once littered the pioneer trails.

A pelican sails slowly out over the water toward the small moored boats, flapping occasionally, and drawing my sight to the horizon. And two feelings come in quick succession. One is the feeling that the sea goes on forever like the starry universe. The other, a feeling that this same eternity is a circle that, in an instant, flashes round the world and ends again with me where I sit. Infinite expanse...infinite finiteness. Only when words are used, do the two feelings seem to conflict with each other.

My attention is brought back to the present by a tourist-- English, perhaps?--who stops to ask how long a walk it is to Cannery Row. As he walks off with his female companion, I notice they are not walking with the same nervous, almost frantic scramble as the others. They are probably in love...

Within a minute, a roar begins and grows louder until a group of jets flying in diamond formation appears and finally flies directly overhead with a thundering shout. It seems as if this is man's answer to the wordless question lapping gently below me. But soon the shriek dies out, and the quiet of the sea returns. And there remains no question as to who has won.

Chapter Eight

What an Inner Agreement Object is Not

Objects have been used for various spiritual or supernatural reasons by humans for time immemorial. I'd like now, to take a look at the most common types, in order to differentiate them from an object you might "use" as a result of The Inner Agreement.

Comfort Objects

The first type is actually used for its psychological benefits: A Comfort Object of Transitional Object is an item used to provide psychological comfort, especially in stressful situations, or at bedtime for small children. It often takes the form of a stuffed animal or blanket.

This object differs from an Inner Agreement object, as its main purpose is to provide comfort and pacification. By its very nature it's rather large, and serves no utilitarian purpose, as I believe any Inner Agreement object would.

Amulets

Another type is the amulet or talisman, which would be used to protect its owner from harm. This object could take many forms, but again, it is not usually, in itself, utilitarian. This type of object is chose because of tradition or religious belief, so is "outwardly" chosen. An Inner Agreement object is chosen internally from reasons arising from the inner psyche. There is no belief in evil, or intention to ask for protection involved.

The pocket knife I chose that helped with anxiety was not in itself very dangerous. But I use it almost every day because I'm involved with maintenance and repair. I feel that it links in some deep way with man's pride at creating tools, and thus making him more self-reliant and confident.

Good Luck Charms

Good luck charms are used to bring good fortune to their owners. Again, these objects are used because of superstition, and chosen based on tradition and the recommendation of others who claim to have special knowledge. An Inner Agreement object is inwardly chosen and, rather, is a living symbol of our unique mental and physical abilities.

To choose an object in hopes it will make you lucky or feel better - by reaching for something that you've been told will "work", would be pointless. You need to let the inner self tell you what it needs in its own way.

Fetishes

According to Wikipedia, "a fetish...is an object believed to have supernatural powers, or in particular, a man-made object that has power over others." By its very nature, this kind of object and its use is antithetical to what an Inner Agreement object represents. The use of a fetish implies the presence and availability of the supernatural - and its powers to effect some change in reality. In The Inner Agreement, the sole intent in determining what object the unconscious mind might "need" is to satisfy an innate and ancient desire to have and use a living symbol of human development.

Chapter Nine

A Vast Ocean Within Us: More on the Brain and Consciousness

Freud

Sigmund Freud was the first doctor to propose the existence of an unconscious mind, and that most of the mind's workings were beneath our awareness. He came to the conclusion that our inner conflicts were the result of childhood traumas. To some extent, this is true, but I suggest that at some point in our evolutionary development, our conscious mind lost crucial touch with the unconscious mind, and this was perpetuated through the millennia by ways of thinking that looked for answers for this sense of loss in things like gods, spirits, mythical creatures, etc.

Freud's psychoanalysis sought to tap into inner conflicts, but stopped short of treating the unconscious mind with the respect with which I feel it expects to be treated. Because of this, Freud got mired down in the idea that most inner conflicts arise from sexual confusion.

The unconscious mind is that part of us that is essentially forever somewhat wild. There are many so called tamable animals that will bite, or attack you under certain circumstances. Perhaps that "wild" part of us will never be truly tamable. But if we understand this, we can channel these tendencies in more productive directions.

Jung

Carl Jung, perhaps the most famous of Freud's associates, also saw the exploration of the unconscious mind as being essential to our wholeness. He saw Freud's view of the unconscious at unnecessarily negative. Whereas Freud saw it as a place where repressed emotions and desires are stored, Jung recognized its vastness – and its connection to a larger collective unconscious. He stressed the need to integrate the opposites in our psyches by use of dreams, *active imagination* and free association. (Jung, 1971)

I also value the goal of integration, but feel that my Inner Agreement approach is a dynamic step toward this integration – and that it is something that nearly anyone can try, with little danger of negative side effects. It's a very simple way to establish a connection with the inner self. Only a few major ideas need to be agreed on: 1. That we indeed have an inner self, with its own agenda and language. 2. That this inner self expects to be treated with respect by the outer self. 3. That, with the proper form of request, the inner self will "work with" the outer self to solve problems.

It may be an odd idea that the inner mind, or any part of the mind, for that matter, has innate needs. What would cause this? The philosopher, John Locke, believed that we are born Tabula Rasa – a blank slate, and that no knowledge is innate. (Locke) But recent research has shown that babies are born with many innate problem-solving abilities. (Cosmides and Tooby, 1995; Pinker, 2003) So humans are hardwired at birth to deal with the often chaotic incoming data. To me, this proves that the inner self, or unconscious mind has, from the start, a relationship with the world it encounters at birth. Someday we'll understand much more clearly, but it seems clear already that we carry "knowledge" at the genetic level. No wonder Jung had to conclude that we have a "collective unconscious". It's in our DNA.

Chapter Ten

Reflections and Ramifications

I should reiterate: I'm not a trained psychologist – I'm just an individual who found something that worked. Once I'd experienced the results, I started to wonder if anyone else had come up with a similar process. I still haven't found anything that is similar enough for me to feel that it's *not* worth an effort to share my experience.

What seems clear to me in all of this is that the unconscious mind plays a large role in our lives, that it has its own language, and that we ignore our inner selves at our own peril. The very reason we've been able to reach our level of civilization is because we have and need both parts of our psyche: the conscious and unconscious mind.

To date, after much double checking with my unconscious mind, I've yet to receive any further requests for objects, except, perhaps, my wedding ring. But it doesn't seem to have the same dramatic effect as the first two objects. I've asked my unconscious mind if it wants any specific actions done, but have not received any clear or positive answer.

As it stands, the two things (the pocket knife and the wristwatch) it's asked for represent: 1. A tool that, once mastered, put mankind light years ahead of all other creatures. (Not to mention the fact that not a day goes by when I don't find some need for it.) and 2. An instrument that represents mankind's need to organize his life in time, *and* his ability to perfect the process of time's measurement.

On a personal level, the two objects also seem to bring back feelings of pride, as they represent presents from my parents that made me feel that I was becoming a more responsible young man in their eyes.

This process hasn't completely eliminated anxiety and depression for me. But the difference is significant. I hope to hear from anyone who tries this method, and see if it works for them as well as it's worked for me.

This year I've noticed two major changes that I feel are part of the continuing benefits of my process. In early June I noticed a pronounced lift in mood and creativity. I also noticed that I was less irritable. Even after clear changes over the last few years, I would still get quite angry sometimes, and feel the need to give someone (usually one of my tenants) a "piece of my mind". I had a dream where I was beginning to get angry at someone, when I realized what was happening and automatically "back down" and began to speak more calmly. The same thing began happening in my waking life. It wasn't as if I was telling myself, "Now, Dale, you stop that right now!" It was more like the angry thought would just vaporize and blow away in the wind. That change has largely stuck, and feels like a permanent change.

Another change at the same time came in the form of an increased tolerance in doing certain repetitive clerical tasks in the office that used to bore me to death. That change also stayed firm.

I'm beginning to wonder if the unconscious mind is associated more with the right brain. I know that the right brain is more involved with the visual, and is less verbal. I plan to do more study along these lines.

In this book, and in my self-therapy, I've dealt with two basic issues: anxiety disorder, and depression. I can see the possibilities of expanding the work: perhaps to guilt, loneliness, regret, phobias, etc. Each of these issues would require its own unique line of inquiry. For instance, it occurred to me that the question for loneliness might be, "What can I give you to help you feel more *complete*?" I want to point out that I've chosen questions that express things in a positive way. For anxiety, "What can I give you to help you feel safer?" For depression, "What can I give you to help you feel more hopeful?" I wouldn't ask, "What can I give you to help you feel less afraid?" or "What can I give you to help you feel less hopeless?" Asking this kind of question in negative terms to the unconscious mind would just feed into the negative loop already spinning.

Fear is an innate reaction to danger, so in itself, is not a bad thing. It mobilizes us to action – either fight or flight. But anxiety disorder and PTSD happen when the unconscious mind is unable to let go of its natural reactions. Thousands of years ago the choices were simpler. But now many of us are faced - either in wars, domestically, or in our cities – with no-win scenarios. Depression, I believe, is the natural reaction to the realization that the choices of fight or flight will not solve the problem. But hope is regained when the unconscious mind can realize that the conscious mind is aware of the inner dilemma and willing to work *together* with the unconscious mind to solve the problem. Using my method, that would mean taking the time to allow the unconscious mind to "show" a living symbol that will satisfy its primal needs – at least until a "healing" has occurred between to conscious and unconscious mind.

The unconscious mind is not meant to hang onto painful memories, and be stuck in a constant emergency mode. That would be useless to animals in the wild. So why should we have to settle for an endless loop of painful thoughts and feelings? We *can* resolve these issues by reestablishing a "working" relationship with the inner creature that still exists within us. Rediscover the unique person you are inside. It's guaranteed that no one else will be quite the same in terms of inner needs. You'll need to do the work of self discovery yourself.

The objects my inner mind "requested" were very specific, and substitutes have had no effect at all. So this process will be *very* personal and really can't be commercialized. Your inner mind will probably want something both meaningful *and* useful. It will be easily carried, so it probably won't be a Lear jet or a Maserati.

References and Recommended Reading

Cosmides and Tooby. COGNITIVE ADAPTATIONS. Oxford University Press, 1995

Eagleman, David M. INCOGNITO – THE SECRET LIVES OF THE BRAIN. New York: Pantheon Books, 2011

Jung, C. G. MAN AND HIS SYMBOLS. New York: Dell Publishing Co., Inc., 1968

Jung, C. G. MEMORIES, DREAMS, REFLECTIONS. New York: Vintage Books, 1971

Locke, John. AN ESSAY CONCERNING HUMAN UNDERSTANDING. Oxford University Press, 1979

Mlodinow, Leonard. SUBLIMINAL: HOW YOUR UNCONSCIOUS MIND RULS YOUR BEHAVIOR. Pantheon, 2012

Pinker, Steven. THE BLANK SLATE. Penguin Books, 2003

Temes, Roberta, Ph.D. THE COMPLETE IDIOT'S GUIDE TO HYPNOSIS. Alpha Books, 2000

About the Author

Dale E. Victorine, a native of California, is a composer and apartment manager. He's written piano, vocal, choral, organ, orchestral, and chamber works. Other interests include psychology, history, nature, art, poetry, flute playing, and American ideals. A member of The National Association of Composers, U.S.A., and The Monterey County Composers Forum, he is active in helping produce several concerts of new music a year.